Contents

Introduction

The aim of this book is to provide a broad range of ideas about how to involve parents in early years settings and engage them in their children's learning.

The influential **Effective Provision of Pre-school Education** research[1] found that children who attend settings that encourage high levels of parental engagement achieve more. This is especially true of settings that explain educational aims and provision to parents because it encourages them to take this knowledge home and use it to provide meaningful learning experiences for their children.

Partnership with parents is highlighted in **The Statutory Framework for the Early Years Foundation Stage** as fundamental to ensuring all children achieve their potential:

'Good parenting and high quality early learning together provide the foundation children need to make the most of their abilities and talents as they grow up.'[2]

The Framework sets out clear expectations in terms of what early years professionals should provide for parents. Key workers are expected to forge positive relationships with parents by keeping them informed, as well as actively engaging them in the life of the setting and supporting them in guiding their children's learning at home.

This book is full of practical examples that aim to help practitioners meet these expectations. It contains ideas for how to ensure that parents are well informed about all aspects of their child's provision, from general day-to-day administrative notices to information about curriculum delivery and early learning.

There are ideas for how to make settings more accommodating and welcoming, making parents feel more comfortable, giving them increased confidence and enticing them to get involved. Furthermore, there are suggestions for how to make settings more flexible and open in order to reach as many parents as possible. These include ideas for reaching out to fathers, as well as parents who speak English as an additional language and parents with children with special educational needs or disabilities.

This book is written in recognition of the fact that parents are their children's first and foremost educators. Early years settings are in a great position to help parents and empower them by guiding them to provide good quality learning experiences in the home. Therefore, there are suggestions for how to inform parents about the early years curriculum and effective approaches to teaching and learning. In addition, there are ideas for how to bring parents into the heart of the setting, by helping with activities and contributing to planning and assessment.

fantastic ideas for
involving parents

MARIANNE SARGENT

Published 2013 by Featherstone Education
Bloomsbury Publishing plc
50 Bedford Square, London, WC1B 3DP
www.bloomsbury.com

ISBN 978-1-4081-7955-0

Printed and bound in China by C&C Offset Printing Co. Ltd., Shenzen, Guangdong

This book is produced using paper that is made from wood grown in
managed, sustainable forests. It is natural, renewable and recyclable.
The logging and manufacturing processes conform to the environmental
regulations of the country of origin.

10 9 8 7 6 5 4 3 2 1

To see our full range of titles visit **www.bloomsbury.com**

Acknowledgements
I would like to thank Chinley Community Preschool, High Peak, Derbyshire for
their ideas, which have contributed to this book. Also with thanks to LEYF, Acorn
Childcare Ltd, Medlock Primary School, Manchester and Little Angel's Schoolhouse
for the photographs.

Child protection

Before coming to work in an early years setting parents should be made aware of child protection and health and safety policies. Practitioners should explain toileting and accident procedures, including what to do if a child needs changing, which members of staff are trained in first aid and what to do if a child discloses something sensitive to you that is a child protection issue.

Any parent helper who attends the setting on a regular basis or is likely to be left alone with a child must have been through a vetting process. The Criminal Records Bureau (CRB) has now been replaced by the Disclosure and Barring Service (DBS), and settings are required to seek a DBS certificate in relation to staff and volunteers who will be working with children. Find more information at; **www.gov.uk/government/organisations/disclosure-and-barring-service.**

Photographs of children

Many of the ideas in this book require the use of photos and film of children playing and working in the setting. It is vital that you gain written parental consent before you include any photos or video footage of children on leaflets, the setting website or the virtual learning environment (VLE).

[1] Siraj-Blatchford I, Sylva K, Melhuish E, Sammons P and Taggart (2004) *Effective Provision of Pre-school Education [EPPE]*: Final Report. Institute of Education, University of London.

[2] Department for Education (DfE) (2012) *The Statutory Framework for the Early Years Foundation Stage*. Nottingham, DfE Publications.

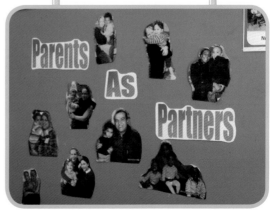

Prospectus

What you need:

- **Computer and printer**

Taking it forward

- Upload the prospectus to the setting's website.
- Add parent testimonials to the prospectus.

What's in it for the parents?

A prospectus is a useful way to ensure that parents are well informed from the very start. It gives parents a sense of confidence in the setting and helps them to feel organised and prepared.

What to do:

1. To inform and advise parents, put together a prospectus about the setting.

   Include:

   - a brief mission statement
   - the aims of the setting
   - admissions policy
   - guidelines regarding clothing and equipment
   - policies regarding sickness, administration of medications, application of sun cream and snow closure
   - information about opening hours and policies regarding what happens if a parent fails to collect their child on time
   - policies with regard to food and snack provision and any payments that might be due
   - an overview of special educational needs and disability policies
   - an overview of the Early Years Foundation Stage (EYFS) areas of learning and development, with examples of the types of activities in which the children will engage
   - photos of the setting
   - staff profiles
   - contact phone numbers.

2. Distribute the prospectus to new and prospective parents.

Home visits

- Plans and staffing arrangements for home visits
- Basket of toys and books
- 'All about me' questionnaire

Taking it forward

- Follow up the initial home visit with more throughout the year to maintain contact with parents who have less opportunity to spend time in the setting.

- If you decide against home visits, send the 'All about me' questionnaires home instead.

What's in it for the parents?

Parents often feel more relaxed and comfortable in their own homes. Home visits help to establish good relationships from the very start by helping practitioners to get to know parents and their children and put them at ease.

Top tip ★

Home visits need careful consideration and planning. The Association of Teachers and Lecturers has produced an information leaflet offering comprehensive advice about the pros and cons involved:
http://www.atl.org.uk/Images/The%20early%20years.pdf

What to do:

1. Before children start at the setting visit them at home. Take a basket of toys and books to share with them.

2. Use the visit to talk with parents and ask them about their children. Prepare an 'All about me' questionnaire based on the following:

   - food likes, dislikes and allergies
   - language development
   - family and special people
   - sleeping patterns
   - comfort routines and comforters
   - fears
   - favourite activities, toys and games
   - medical conditions and medications
   - toileting and self-care skills
   - care arrangements: child minders, other preschools
   - cultural background and religious beliefs
   - involvement of outside agencies.

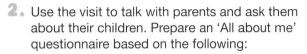

3. Take the opportunity to ask parents about their own feelings about their child starting at the setting. Do they have any worries or anxieties?

Induction

What you need:

- Plans and staffing arrangements for having new starters in the setting
- Time to talk with new parents and children

What to do:

1. Before children start at the setting invite them in to visit. Arrange at least two visits prior to them joining.

2. During the visits talk with parents and ask them about their children. Find out about:

   - favourite activities and games they like to play at home

   - preferences for particular toys

   - their interests

   - how they think their children will feel about the setting and if they foresee any problems or issues.

3. Take the opportunity to show parents around the setting, explain routines and introduce them to other members of staff. Invite them to ask any questions they might have.

Taking it forward

■ When their children start at the setting ask parents to make themselves available for the first two weeks so that they can be on hand for comfort and support. Invite them to come into the setting each day and settle their children in. Explain that they can stay as long as they like and leave when they feel comfortable.

■ Ask parents of children who already attend the setting to come in and spend time with new parents.

What's in it for the parents?

Parents will feel more comfortable and at ease if they are given time to become familiar with the setting and staff.

My family

What you need:

- Display board
- Photographs of children and their families

My family

Josh and his baby brother

Sally and her granny

Ben and his dog Harry

What to do:

1. Ask parents to send in photos of their children with significant family members with notes on the back about who everyone is.

2. Create a 'My family' display featuring each of the children and their family members.

3. Ask the children about the photos. Put captions with the photos naming everyone and adding the children's comments.

Taking it forward

- Arrange an open morning when parents are invited to bring children's siblings in for a play.

- Organise an open day when other family members are invited to come along and visit the setting.

What's in it for the parents?

This is a nice 'getting to know you' activity during the induction period, serving as a springboard for opening up conversation between practitioners and parents.

Meeting individual needs

What you need:

- **Time and staffing arrangements to enable you to meet with parents**

Taking it forward

- Regularly meet with the parents to review the original decisions and plans, and to discuss any changing needs.

- Talk to the children concerned and ask them for their views and suggestions.

What's in it for the parents?

It is good practice to make time to listen to all parents and learn about their children's individual needs and wants. However, it is especially important to ensure that parents with children with disabilities or special educational needs are included in planning and decision-making. This will help these parents feel supported and ensure their child receives the care they need and deserve.

What to do:

1. Invite parents of children with disabilities or special educational needs to meet with you to discuss how the setting can provide for their needs. Ask for the parents' input with regard to:

   - how the physical environment can be arranged or altered to make negotiating space and accessing resources easier

   - toileting arrangements

   - how signs and labeling might be displayed or positioned to make them more helpful

   - behaviour management strategies used at home

   - equipment or resources that might be useful

   - organisations that might offer financial assistance in terms of purchasing special equipment or resources

   - recommended books or literature about their child's particular condition or need.

Website

What you need:

- Computer
- Access to the internet

What to do:

1. Set up a website for the setting. Use a free easy-to-use service like Classtell (classtell.com) or WordPress (wordpress.com).

2. Use the website to:

   - share the setting's prospectus and policies
   - distribute newsletters
   - provide contact details
   - post important notices, for example, closure due to snow
   - share Ofsted reports
   - advise parents about term dates
   - highlight important diary dates
   - provide information about current topics or projects
   - post photos of children involved in activities
   - provide links to useful websites.

Taking it forward

- Set up a Facebook page and Twitter account for the setting. Use them to post important information and urgent notices that need to reach parents quickly.

- Use a texting service to send out important messages and reminders.

What's in it for the parents?

A website is a very useful way of keeping parents informed. This is particularly important for parents who work long hours and whose children attend after school care or are collected by child minders. It is easy for letters to get mislaid and most parents will have regular access to the internet at home.

Staying safe

- Ensure your website is password protected.

- Get parents' written consent before posting photos of their children on the website.

- Facebook and Twitter accounts should be assigned an administrator who is responsible for monitoring them regularly to remove any dubious or potentially offensive posts. Do not use Facebook to share surnames or photos of the children and ensure privacy settings are set to private to ensure only 'friends' are able to view information.

Information evening

What you need:

- Time during an evening
- Example photo and video observations
- Digital photo frames or electronic tablets (optional)
- Interactive whiteboard (optional)

Top tip ⭐

Set up a supervised play area for children whose parents need childcare to enable them to attend.

What to do:

1. Invite parents in for an information evening.

2. Prepare a presentation featuring photo observations and use it to explain what learning in the early years looks like.

3. Set out toys and activities with accompanying explanations about the learning and development opportunities that they offer. Use digital photo frames or electronic tablets to show pictures of the children playing in different areas of the setting or print out captioned photos and stick them in the relevant places.

4. Play some video of children involved in an investigation on the interactive whiteboard.

5. Make setting staff available to verbally explain the resources and activities and answer parents' questions.

Taking it forward

- Produce an information booklet that parents can take home and share with partners and family members.

What's in it for the parents?

Informing parents about learning and development in the early years will help them to support their children at home.

Parents' noticeboard

What you need:

- **Noticeboard** (positioned somewhere easily accessed by parents)

What to do:

1. Set up a parents' noticeboard that is positioned in the cloakroom area or a place that is easily accessed by parents.

2. Use the noticeboard to:
   - display the weekly planning
   - display current newsletters
   - post important notices
   - post reminders about forthcoming events
   - provide information about current topics or projects
   - show what snack is on offer each day.

Taking it forward

- Set up a website for posting more detailed and comprehensive information.
- Allocate a section of the noticeboard for parents to post their own notices.

What's in it for the parents?

A noticeboard is helpful for keeping parents informed about what is happening in the setting on a day-to-day basis. It is easy for parents to check on the way in and out, helping to keep them organised. Furthermore, allocating space for parents to use the board gives them a sense of ownership.

The EYFS on display

What to do:

1. Put up a display explaining the aims, themes and principles of the EYFS.

2. Explain what the characteristics of effective learning are and use photo observations to illustrate.

3. Explain the rationale behind having three prime areas and four specific areas of learning and development. Describe what each area covers.

Taking it forward

- Put together an information leaflet about the EYFS and send it home for parents to read in their own time.

What's in it for the parents?

Informing parents about the EYFS will make them better equipped to talk to practitioners and ask questions about their children's learning and development. It will also help them to better understand their children's assessment profiles.

Play date

What you need:

- Computer, printer and laminator
- Your copy of *Development Matters in the Early Years Foundation Stage*

What to do:

1. Send out letters inviting parents in for a 'play date'.

2. Set out a good range of toys, games and resources to show parents what their children do when they attend the setting.

3. Next to each resource display an information card explaining:
   - what the resource is
   - the areas of learning and development children experience while playing with it
   - what knowledge and skills the children develop while playing with it
   - how developing such knowledge and skills lays the foundations for future learning.

4. Allow parents to wander around the setting and invite them to examine and play with the toys, games and resources with their children.

5. Join in the play, talk to the parents and answer their questions.

Taking it forward

- Ask parents if they have any ideas or suggestions for different toys, games and resources they think might be beneficial to the children.

What's in it for the parents?

Inviting parents in to play not only informs them about the ways in which young children learn it also breaks down barriers, making them feel welcome to enter the setting and approach practitioners.

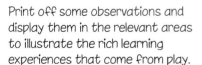

Top tip ★

Print off some observations and display them in the relevant areas to illustrate the rich learning experiences that come from play.

Parents' room

What to do:

1. Set up a parents' room with seating, a kettle and supply of tea and coffee.

2. Make the room freely accessible to parents to meet and talk.

3. Arrange for setting staff to take turns to pop into the room from time-to-time, check in with the parents and have a chat.

Taking it forward

- Put leaflets and displays up around the room with information about local services.

- Talk to parents about the possibility of setting up a parenting group that might like to meet in the parents' room.

What's in it for the parents?

A parents' room provides a base where parents can come together and socialise, helping them to forge relationships with each other. In addition, it is an informal setting where practitioners can engage with parents to find out their opinions, views and needs.

Coffee morning

What you need:

- Tea, coffee, decaffeinated alternatives, milk, sugar, sweeteners and biscuits
- Kettle or electric urn and cups
- Space to create a serving and seating area for the parents

What to do:

1. Set a date and invite parents and carers in for a coffee morning.

2. On the day put out a range of toys and resources for the children and set up a seating area for parents.

3. Use the morning as an opportunity to listen to parents' stories about their children and to give them a chance to ask questions and make comments about the setting.

4. Encourage the children to show their parents around and tell them about what they have been doing.

Taking it forward

- Hold regular coffee mornings, perhaps once every half term.

What's in it for the parents?

Events like this make parents feel welcome and comfortable in the setting. It gives them an opportunity to talk about their children in an informal situation and build relationships with members of staff. Furthermore, it gives them time to look around the environment and wall displays.

Health & Safety

Ensure hot drinks are served and drunk in an allocated area where there is no risk of spillage near the children.

Support services

What you need:

- A reasonably large additional room to accommodate visiting users

What to do:

1. Invite other agencies to use your setting to provide early years services. For example:
   - midwife/health visitor
   - local parent and toddler group
   - baby massage
   - baby sign
   - music group
   - anti-natal group
   - parenting classes.

Taking it forward

- Ask parents if there are any services that they would be interested in attending.
- Invite the parents to use the room to set up groups of their own, for example a father's group or breastfeeding circle.

What's in it for the parents?

Parents are more likely to access activities and services if they are provided at a convenient place and time. Furthermore, inviting other agencies into your setting helps to create a sense of community by introducing parents to practitioners and other early years professionals as well as each other.

Flexi-time

What you need:

- **Arrangements for flexible staffing and opening hours**

What to do:

1. Make your setting more accessible and welcoming by extending opening hours and making staff available for longer at the beginning and end of each session. Some ideas include:

   - Make it clear that you have an open door policy so that parents feel they are welcome to approach practitioners.

   - Have a member of staff on the door at the beginning and end of each day to meet and greet parents, receive day-to-day information or answer any questions they might have.

   - Plan for staff to work a four-day week in rotation, enabling them to take turns to be available for an extra hour before the start and after the finish of each session.

   - Introduce a flexible start time, for example between 8am and 9.30am, so that arrivals are staggered, giving practitioners more time to speak to individual parents.

   - Set out resources for children to come in and play with as soon as they arrive while parents and practitioners talk.

Taking it forward

- If possible try to arrange for bilingual staff to be on hand to translate at the beginning and end of each session. If not, find out if there are any parents who would be happy to help.

What's in it for the parents?

Being flexible accommodates the needs of more parents, making it more likely that they will engage with the setting.

Focus groups

What you need:

- Time to meet and talk with parents

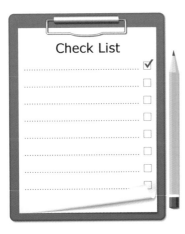

Check List

What to do:

1. Invite parents to attend focus group meetings to discuss how best to communicate with and involve them.

2. Ask the parents which form of communication they find most useful: letter, email, verbal, text or post on the website. Would they prefer certain types of communication depending on the reason? For example, text for urgent notices and letters for general information.

3. Ask if they would like to be involved in the setting and if so, in what way.

4. See if they have any questions about the early years' curriculum and if they do, find out what the setting could do or provide to help them learn more.

Taking it forward

- Send out questionnaires to those parents who are unable to attend focus group meetings.

- Put a suggestions box near the entrance to the setting for parents to post requests and ideas.

What's in it for the parents?

A good starting point when evaluating how best to communicate with and involve parents is to simply ask them. This shows them you are willing to listen and accommodate their needs, making it easier for them to get involved.

Visual timetable

What you need:

- Five large pieces of stiff card
- An A-board or flipchart easel
- Digital camera
- Computer and printer
- Sticky back plastic

What to do:

1. Throughout the course of a week take photos of children involved in regular activities, routines and events. For example, morning registration, story times, circle times and music and movement.

2. Use one piece of card for each day of the week. Mount the photos on the cards in time order to show what happens during that particular session or day in the setting.

3. Add simple captions, for example: 'Mid-morning we come together on the carpet for brain gym to exercise our bodies and minds.'

4. Laminate the cards with sticky back plastic.

5. Each day display the relevant card for parents and children to see.

Taking it forward

- Leave blank spaces on the timetable for adding details of any focus activities, project work or last minute events. As the cards are laminated, this can be done either by writing on them with board markers or by sticking paper on with sticky tack.

- Include photos of children holding up the 'five more minutes' timer, shaking the bells to call everyone together or lining up for lunch. These pictures might be accompanied by a caption: 'When we hear the bells we know it is time to sit on the carpet.' This shares setting behaviour management strategies with parents and gives them ideas that they might like to use at home.

- Create an, 'Our day at pre-school' display.

What's in it for the parents?

A visual timetable set up in the cloakroom area not only gives children a sense of security, it also informs parents about the setting's daily routines.

Home communication books

What you need:

- A small notebook for each child

Taking it forward

- Use setting-to-setting communication books that can be passed between your setting and any others that the child may attend. This will help to build a more rounded picture of the child and inform you of their aptitudes and interests in different settings, as well as any important issues.

What's in it for the parents?

A home communication book helps practitioners maintain a regular dialogue with parents. This is especially useful in large busy settings or in the case of children who are collected by family members or child minders. Key workers might not have the opportunity to speak to parents on a daily basis and can use the book to give them regular updates on progress.

Top tip ★

Use text messaging to send daily updates to parents who are unable to drop off and pick up their children.

What to do:

1. Prepare a small notebook for each child in the setting. In the front cover of the book put an explanation of what the book is for. For example:

   This is your child's home-setting communication book. It will be sent home every Friday. Please return it on the following Monday. Your child's key worker will use the book to pass along interesting information about what your child has been doing during the week. They may also use it to highlight achievements or to ask questions. Please feel free to add your response and use the book to pass information back to us.

2. Use the notebooks to:

   - tell parents about their children's achievements
   - ask questions about children's likes/dislikes
   - comment on something interesting a child has said or done
   - remind parents about an upcoming event.

What you need:

- Access to online translators

What to do:

1. Make your setting as accessible as possible by asking parents and other members of staff from different ethnic backgrounds to help you add translations to labelling and notices. A useful website is **www.freetranslation.com**.

2. Translate display titles, room labels and welcome signs. Find a multilingual welcome poster from Bright Ideas: **www.brightideasteaching.co.uk**.

3. Display translated versions of the visual timetable and daily notices.

What's in it for the parents?

Offering translations of labelling, letters and literature is a good way of reaching out to parents who may feel alienated by a language barrier. For parents who are new to the country and as yet unable to speak English, it will help them during the settling in period. On a practical note, it will also ensure that all parents have equal access to important notices or information.

Taking it forward

- Over time, put together a file of translated standard letters and information sheets in different languages. Do the same for your setting's prospectus.

- If it's not possible to translate letters, keep the text short and snappy, incorporate pictures and take those parents who are able to understand spoken English aside to verbally explain the main points.

- Ask parents to teach you some simple words and phrases in their language, for example, 'Good morning' and 'How are you?'

- Put together a collection of stories with bilingual texts to send home with parents and children who speak English as an additional language.

Learning stories

What you need:

- Digital camera
- Clipboards, notebooks, sticky notes, pens

What to do:

1. Throughout the course of a topic, project or investigation take photos of the children's activities.

2. Record the children's comments.

3. When the project or investigation is complete, put together a learning story:
   - choose a format: picture book, information book or comic strip
   - insert the photos and tell the story of what the children did and learned by adding a narrative, quotations, speech bubbles, captions or information boxes.

4. Print off the learning story and bind it to create a book.

5. Share the learning story with the children before sending it home to parents.

The dough is squashy

Peter used a rolling pin to roll out the dough.

We had lots of different shaped cutters. Peter liked the heart shape best.

I made a bell!

We put the biscuits on a baking tray.

Then we baked them in the oven to make them hard and crunchy.

Taking it forward

- Invite the children to add to the narrative, suggest captions and offer comments to fill in speech bubbles.

- Attach a form to the back of the story for parents to give feedback.

- Attach some ideas for open questions that parents can ask their children about the story.

- Create the learning story using presentation software like PowerPoint or Photo Story 3 and upload it to the setting website or VLE.

What's in it for the parents?

Learning stories are a fun way to show parents what their children have been doing. Furthermore, the story format makes them ideal for parents to share with their children, opening up opportunities for them to talk and reflect together.

More information

Find an example of a learning story, as well as more ideas for sharing learning with parents in *The Project Approach: Creativity in the Early Years* by Marianne Sargent (Practical Pre-School Books).

Look what we have done today

What you need:

- Digital camera
- Digital photo frame, iPad or electronic tablet

Taking it forward

- If using an iPad use an app such as iCaption to enable you to add captions to the photos. These might include a brief explanation of the activity or things the children have said.

- Allocate a space in the setting where children can leave work in progress. Encourage children to bring their parents in to see what they have been doing.

- Create 'We are learning about…' displays that feature the current topic or theme.

What's in it for the parents?

This is a lovely way to show parents what their children have been doing in the setting each day and opens up opportunities for parents to initiate conversations with their children about the activities they have been involved in.

Top tip ★

There are many free apps that enable you to add captions to photos. Just search the app store for your particular tablet.

What to do:

1. Take photos of the children throughout each session or day.

2. Upload the photos to a digital photo frame or electronic tablet.

3. Set the frame or tablet to show the photos as a slideshow and put it in the cloakroom area for parents to watch while they wait to drop off or collect their children.

4. If you do not have access to a digital photo frame or electronic tablet, simply print the photos and bind or staple them together to make a book.

5. Otherwise use a permanent ring binder file entitled, 'Look what we have done today' and insert a new set of photos each day.

6. Make sure that every child is featured in the photos at least once every couple of days.

Wow wall!

What you need:

- Photographs of all the children in the setting
- Computer, printer and laminator
- Sticky notes

What to do:

1. Take close up photos of each of the children in the setting.

2. Laminate the photos and mount them on a display in the cloakroom area or somewhere easily accessed by parents.

3. During the course of the day collect snapshot observations of the children on sticky notes and keep the more significant observations to one side.

4. Stick the notes that highlight particular achievements on the relevant children's photos before the end of the session.

5. Direct parents to the 'Wow wall!' when they come to collect their children.

6. Try to ensure you stick at least one note on each child's photo every week.

Taking it forward

- Leave a pad of sticky notes and a pen near the wall and invite parents to add their children's 'wow' moments from home.

What's in it for the parents?

This is a great way to build a sense of achievement in the children and gives parents an opportunity to share in their successes. It is also a good way of demonstrating to parents how practitioners observe their children and take note of each individual achievement they make as they progress along their individual learning journeys.

Top tip ★

Keep a tick list of children and make a note of the date each time you attach a sticky note on the wall to help you keep track and prevent you from missing anyone out.

WOW!

Cara counted to 10

Sanya completed a 6 piece jigsaw

Sanya made some cakes

James built a robot out of boxes

Ellie knew we needed flour to make a cake

Learning profiles

What you need:

- Ring binders or A4 project books

What to do:

1. Create a learning profile for each child in the setting. Use it to present:
   - tracking observations
   - photos with accompanying observation notes
   - focused observations
   - snapshot observations.

2. Insert record sheets detailing the child's current level of attainment in each of the areas of learning and development.

3. Send the children's learning profiles home at least once a term for parents to look though.

Taking it forward

- Place a summary record at the front of the files providing an overview of each child's achievements as well as suggestions for next steps in each area of learning and development. Use parent-friendly language and provide a space for the parents to comment.

What's in it for the parents?

Sending learning profiles home reinforces parents' position as partners of the setting. A detailed file containing a range of photo observations will help parents to understand their children better, often highlighting issues that they may not have noticed at home. Sharing this knowledge puts parents in a stronger position to deliver their role as foremost educators of their children.

Parent consultations

What you need:

- Staffing arrangements to enable each key worker to meet with parents
- Children's learning profiles

Taking it forward

- Arrange phone consultations for parents unable to attend.

- Create an e-portfolio that can be sent via email. Use presentation software such as PowerPoint to put together an electronic learning profile of the child's learning and development. Include observations, photos and film. Email this home to parents and ask for their views, comments and questions.

What's in it for the parents?

Parents need time to talk about their children and it is not always possible to speak to everyone on a daily basis. Setting time aside to hold individual consultations gives parents the individual time and attention they need.

Top tip ★

- Give parents a range of options for attending consultations. Offer morning, afternoon and evening sessions in order to accommodate their varying work and childcare commitments.

- Spread consultations over a number of weeks to make it possible to give parents more time while placing less pressure on key workers.

What to do:

1. Hold consultations once every term where parents can meet with their child's key worker.

2. Send each child's learning profile home about a week before the consultation.

3. Include a letter to accompany the profile explaining that there will be an opportunity for them to attend parent consultations.

4. Put up a list of dates and times with space for parents to sign up for the most convenient time.

5. Remind parents the day before their consultation.

6. Allow 30 minutes for each consultation:

   - Begin by highlighting the areas of learning and development that the child enjoys and achieves within most.

   - Move on to point out the areas within which the child needs support.

   - Explain upcoming topics and themes and consult with the parents to create a learning plan based around these as well as the child's interests and needs.

   - Give parents ideas for what they can do to help support their children at home.

   - Ask the parents for their views. What do they think and how do they feel about what you have told them? Do they have anything to add? Can they make any suggestions about how to handle certain situations? Do they have any questions?

Virtual learning environment

What you need:

- Computer
- Access to the internet
- Funding to set up a VLE
- **Some IT knowhow** (or help from someone who is IT savvy)

What to do:

1. Take some time to research VLE platforms. The following are commercial providers that specialise in primary and early years education:

Learnanywhere: **www.learnanywhere.co.uk**

Frog Primary: **www.frogtrade.com** and **www.exa-networks.co.uk**

School VLE: **www.schoolvle.co.uk**

School Spider: **www.schoolspider.co.uk**

My Learning UK: **www.mylearningltd.co.uk**

LifeParents by Uniservity: **www.uniservity.com**

Or try free web application:
Moodle: **www.moodle.org**

2. Set up your VLE and use it to upload resources that parents can access and use with their children. For example:

- Links to websites that feature interactive and animated stories, such as the British Council: **www.britishcouncil.org** and kidSMART: **www.kidsmart.org.uk**

- Links to websites that feature educational games, such as Cbeebies: **www.bbc.co.uk/cbeebies** and Primary Resources: **www.primaryresources.co.uk**

- Information pages and fact sheets about a current topic with links to child-friendly websites so that parents can help their children with research

- Links to software used in the setting

- Games and activities that you have created using 2DIY or interactive whiteboard software such as SMART Notebook or ActivPrimary

Taking it forward

- Use the VLE to display children's work and creations. Upload photos and scan in pieces of artwork.

- Post photos and video of the children working and playing in the setting with space for parents to add comments.

- Start up blogs about topics or setting events for parents to discuss.

- Find out if your local authority subscribes to *Child's Eye Channel* or similar and set up a link from the VLE for parents and children to access a range of child-friendly documentaries.

- Send digital cameras or digital blue video cameras home with the children. Upload their photos and videos to their individual learning journals on the VLE and ask parents to input explanations and comments.

What's in it for the parents?

A VLE makes it possible for parents to get directly involved with their children's learning. This is especially useful for parents who have work commitments and are unable to help out in the setting. It is also a useful platform for parents to communicate with practitioners and each other.

Staying safe

- Ensure your VLE is password protected and regularly monitored.

- Get parents' written consent before posting photos or video of their children on the VLE.

- Advice for practitioners on internet safety can be found from the UK Safer Internet Centre: **www.saferinternet.org.uk** and the NSPCC: **www.nspcc.org.uk/Inform/resourcesforprofessionals/onlinesafety/internet-safety-schools_wda94003.html**.

- Find a good example of a home-user agreement produced by Carisbrooke CE Primary School with child-friendly language for young children at: **www.school-portal.co.uk/GroupDownloadFile.asp?GroupID=1233747&ResourceId=4797909**.

- Include a page for parents with web links offering advice on keeping their children safe on the internet such as CEOP's Thinkuknow: **www.thinkuknow.co.uk/parents** and CBBC's Stay Safe: **www.bbc.co.uk/cbbc/topics/stay-safe**

Lending Library

What you need:

- A selection of story and information books
- A selection of games
- A selection of laminated rhyme cards with puppets and props
- Notebook and pen
- Plastic zip-up wallets
- A4 paper
- Scissors and glue

Top tip ⭐

Have a member of staff or parent volunteer on hand to sign books in and out to help keep track of who has borrowed what.

What to do:

1. Set up a lending library of books, rhymes and games for parents to borrow and take home.

2. Choose books that feature rhythmical, repetitive text with rhyme and alliteration. Include some traditional tales and a good selection of non-fiction books. Ensure there is a wide variety to choose from. Some good examples are:

The Gruffalo by Julia Donaldson (Macmillan)

Handa's Surprise by Eileen Browne (Walker)

Elmer by David McKee (Andersen)

Building Site by Felicity Brooks (Usborne Lift and Look)

The Little Red Train: Faster, Faster! by Benedict Blathwayt (Red Fox)

The Very Busy Spider by Eric Carle (Puffin)

Dazzling Diggers by Tony Mitton and Ant Parker (Kingfisher)

We're Going on a Bear Hunt by Michael Rosen and Helen Oxenbury (Walker)

Dinosaurs by Stephanie Turnbull (Usborne Beginners)

Dear Zoo by Rod Campbell (Macmillan)

Peepo! by Janet and Allen Ahlberg (Puffin)

Emergency! by Margaret Mayo and Alex Ayliffe (Orchard)

Peace at Last by Jill Murphy (Macmillan)

One Snowy Night by Nick Butterworth (HarperCollins)

Farmyard Tales: Noisy Tractor by Sam Taplin and Stephen Cartwright (Usborne)

Guess How Much I Love You by Sam McBratney and Anita Jeram (Walker)

The Three Billy Goat's Gruff by Stephen Tucker and Nick Sharratt (Macmillan)

3. Gather a selection of games that parents can play with their children. Choose games that develop memory, counting, thinking, turn taking, listening and attention skills. Find good resources from retailers including:

Orchard Toys: **www.orchardtoys.com**

TTS: **www.tts-group.co.uk**

Early Learning Centre: **www.elc.co.uk**

Otherwise make them by hand using the following websites for help:

TES Connect: **www.tes.co.uk**

KidSparkz: **www.kidsparkz.com**

Enchanted Learning: **www.enchantedlearning.com**

4. Type out some rhymes and laminate them. Source some puppets and props to go with them. Find a range of nursery rhyme finger puppets from

The Puppet Company: **www.thepuppetcompany.com** and Madeleine Lindley Ltd: **www.madeleinelindley.com**

5. Put the books, rhymes and games in plastic zip-up wallets with accompanying resources.

6. Include laminated cards with hints and tips for sharing them at home.

7. Set up the library in an easily accessible area and provide a notebook and pen for parents to sign them out.

Taking it forward

- As time goes on add extra resources. For example, recipe cards to go with books featuring food, cuddly bears to go with stories about bears, or audio versions of stories and rhymes on CD.

- Ask parents for suggestions about what they would like to be able to borrow.

What's in it for the parents?

A lending library is useful for parents who might otherwise be unable to afford many books and games of their own. It is also more convenient than travelling to a library and there is the added bonus of guidance from practitioners about how to use the resources.

More information

Lawrence Educational: **www.lawrenceeducational.com**, has produced a range of resources specifically for parents, carers and child minders.

Role-play boxes

What you need:

- Durable storage boxes with lids
- Resources and books related to each theme

What to do:

1. Create a set of role-play boxes that parents can borrow and take home to play with their children. Give each box a theme. For example:

   - **Emergency:** fire fighter or police costumes and accessories, laminated pictures of fire fighters and police at work, books such as *Emergency!* (Big Noisy Book) by Ladybird.

   - **Doctor:** white coat, medical instruments, appointment book, pictures of doctors, hospitals and x-rays; books such as *Topsy and Tim Go To The Doctor* by Jean and Gareth Adamson (Ladybird).

   - **Holidays:** travel tickets, suitcase, clothing for different weathers, beach toys, travel magazines, pictures of aeroplanes, boats, trains and coaches, books such as *Spot Goes on Holiday* by Eric Hill (Puffin).

   - **Vet:** cuddly toy domestic animals, pet food containers, animal carriers, vet costume and accessories, pictures of vets examining animals, books such as *Vet (People Who Help Us)* by Amanda Askew and Andrew Crowson (QED Publishing).

   - **Shoe shop:** different sized shoes (child and adult), foot-sizer or measuring tape, till, money, laces, shoe boxes, books such as *Lulu's Shoes* by Camilla Reid and Ailie Busby (Bloomsbury).

2. Put information cards in each box listing the contents, offering suggestions for play scenarios and providing key words and open questions parents can ask during the play.

3. Put an additional information card in explaining how role-play is beneficial to early learning and where it fits into the EYFS.

Taking it forward

■ Ask parents and children for more ideas for role-play boxes and donations toward creating them.

What's in it for the parents?

Role-play boxes are a good way of encouraging parents to play with their children and helping them find out about the value of play as a learning experience.

More information

Find ideas for putting some role-play boxes together in *The Little Book of Prop Boxes for Role Play* by Ann Roberts (Featherstone).

Activity booklet

What you need:

- Computer and printer

Top tip ⭐

Include a good range of activities; some that need planning but also a good selection that are simple and straightforward. This is to enable parents to dip into the booklet at a moment's notice and find something to do.

Taking it forward

- Invite parents to take photos of the activities for children to bring in and share with the setting.

- Ask parents for suggestions about good activities that can be included in the booklet.

What's in it for the parents?

Activity booklets give parents ideas for valuable learning experiences they can provide at home. They also help to illustrate to parents how they may already be fostering their children's learning during the everyday activities they do.

What to do:

1. Put together a booklet of activities that parents can do with their children at home.

2. For each suggestion give a description of the activity and any resources they will need. Provide ideas for questions parents can ask their children and key vocabulary they can introduce while involved in the activities. In addition, include an explanation of how each activity fosters their children's learning.

3. Some ideas for activities include:

   - cooking up a vegetable stew or fruit salad

   - growing a sunflower or tomato plant

   - making home-made play dough

   - creating a pop-up card for a special occasion

   - building a den

   - making Easter eggs

   - going on a minibeast hunt

   - rock pool fishing

   - making pasta collages

   - going on listening walks

   - setting up an obstacle course in the garden

   - making a pirate ship using the living room furniture.

Story bags

What you need:

- Drawstring bags
- A variety of picture books
- Games, puppets and resources to accompany each book

What to do:

1. Create a set of story bags that parents can borrow and take home to use with their children. Suggestions for contents include:
   - a picture book
   - audio version of the book
   - games
   - puppets
   - items related to the story
   - natural objects
   - sensory objects
   - music CD.

2. Put information cards in each bag listing the contents, offering ideas for discussion points and suggesting key words and open questions parents can ask during the story.

Taking it forward

- Ask parents for more ideas for story bags and donations toward creating them.

- Visit children's homes with story bags to read and play with children. During the visits listen to parents and invite them to talk about any general issues and concerns they might have.

What's in it for the parents?

Sharing stories is an invaluable experience for both children and parents and story bags provide parents with all the inspiration and resources they need to extend the fun.

More information

- Find ideas about how to make your own story bags in *The Little Book of Story Bags* by Marianne Sargent (Featherstone).

- Buy ready-made story bags from **www.storysack.com**.

Literacy and maths booklets

What you need:

- Computer and printer

Taking it forward

- Set up subject-based parent working parties, where parents and practitioners come together to talk about what children are doing in the setting and at home. Devise and plan literacy and maths activities together, go away to try them out and then meet up again to share your findings.

- Put together literacy and maths boxes containing games and activity ideas that parents can borrow.

- Put up literacy and maths displays explaining how these subjects are taught in the early years.

What's in it for the parents?

Providing an explanation about literacy and maths in the EYFS is a good idea because it informs parents about what and how their children are learning in these specific areas. This helps parents to understand why their children are engaging in playful activities that develop essential pre-skills before moving on to more formal education. It also guides parents and helps them to choose age-appropriate learning activities at home.

What to do:

1. For children in the Reception year produce a literacy and a maths booklet to inform parents about how these subjects are taught in the early years.

2. Inside each booklet provide:

    - An explanation of the subject as set out in the EYFS. Explain the skills and knowledge that children are expected to learn in the early years.

    - Examples of the types of activities that the setting provides to support the learning of literacy and maths skills.

    - Photos and short observations to illustrate this.

    - Ideas for age-appropriate games and activities that parents can do at home with their children to support their learning in these subjects.

Technology day

What you need:

- Interactive whiteboard
- Computers
- Light box
- Digital cameras and video cameras
- Listening centre, headphones and microphones
- Digital microscope
- Programmable toys

What to do:

1. Invite parents in for a technology day.
2. Set up a range of technology equipment around the setting. For example:
   - **interactive whiteboard:** interactive games
   - **computers:** setting website and/or VLE, software such as 2Simple or Early Years World
   - **light box:** coloured glass pebbles, coloured geo shapes, x-ray slides
   - **digital cameras and video cameras**
   - **listening centre:** stories, rhymes, music and listening games
   - **digital microscope:** leaves, pinecones, shells, fabric swatches
   - **programmable toys:** Bee-Bot, Constructa-Bot, remote controlled vehicles.
3. Invite parents to examine and try out the equipment.
4. Be on hand to show parents how to use the equipment, explain what it is used for and what the children learn when using it.
5. Take the opportunity to show parents around the setting's website or VLE.

Taking it forward

- Invite the children to show their parents what they are able to do with the equipment.
- Ask parents if they would be interested in attending a computer skills workshop.

What's in it for the parents?

Inviting parents in to explore the technology used in the setting serves two purposes. As well as showing them what their children are learning, it gives them an opportunity to try the technology out and learn how to use it themselves. This empowers parents by developing their technological knowledge and skills.

Activity boxes

Taking it forward

- Ask parents for more ideas for activity boxes and donations toward creating them.
- Create a set of themed treasure boxes. Find inspiration in *The Little Book of Treasure Boxes* by Pat Brunton and Linda Thornton (Featherstone) and *The Little Book of Treasure Baskets* by Ann Roberts (Featherstone).

What's in it for the parents?

Activity boxes provide parents with inspiration to set up valuable learning experiences they can share with their children at home.

What to do:

1. Create a set of activity boxes that parents can borrow and take home to use with their children. Give each box a theme. For example:

   - **Cooking:** recipe cards, utensils, books such as *Tasty Poems* by Jill Bennett and Nick Sharratt (Oxford University Press).

   - **Gardening:** seeds, planting tools, stories such as *The Tiny Seed* by Eric Carle (Picture Puffin).

   - **Traditional tales:** story cards, puppets, props, audio CDs such as *Nursery Tales* read by Victoria Wood (HarperCollins).

   - **Arts and crafts:** paints, craft papers, glue, glitter, pencils, chalks, pictures of art works by famous artists.

   - **Music:** musical instruments, selection of CDs representing a variety of genres.

   - **Investigation:** magnifiers, microscopes, cameras, binoculars, bug viewers, pond nets, containers, notebooks.

2. Put information cards in each box listing the contents, offering ideas for activities and suggesting key words parents can use and 'open' questions they can ask during the activities.

3. Put a diary or note pad in each box for parents to share their experiences of using the boxes with each other and practitioners.

Send a project home

What you need:

- This will depend on what you decide to send home for each project

Top tip ⭐

Help parents by sending home an accompanying letter with ideas and tips for how to complete the project.

Taking it forward

- Ask parents if they have any ideas for home projects.

- Invite parents to bring the project back in and share the results with everyone.

What's in it for the parents?

Sending home projects and challenges is a good way of directly involving parents in topics so they can share learning experiences with their children.

What to do:

1. Send a project home for parents to complete with their children. Tie it into the current topic or theme.

2. Suggestions for projects are:

    - Get the children to plant a seed and send it home for parents to help them grow it into a plant.

    - Send home a challenge to make a boat that floats and invite parents in for a model boat gala.

    - Ask parents to help their children make a kite and invite them on an outing to the park to test them out.

    - Host a 'bake off'. Ask parents to bake a cake with their children and invite them in for judging.

    - Involve parents in making costumes for performances or project events, for example a space suit for a trip to the moon.

Family photo books

What you need:

- Digital or disposable cameras
- Notebooks
- A5 card
- Materials to bind the card to create a book
- Computer, printer and laminator

What to do:

1. Send cameras home with the children and ask parents to take photos to record the events of family activities and outings.

2. Provide notebooks for parents to provide captions to accompany the photos.

3. When the cameras and notebooks are returned print off the photos and mount them on the cards. Add the captions provided by the parents to the photos.

4. Laminate the cards and bind them together to create storybooks.

5. Send the books home for parents to read with their children.

Taking it forward

- Send an important toy character from the setting home for weekends with different children in turn. Give the toy a small suitcase or rucksack containing a camera and notebook for parents to record the events of their stay.

- Once the parents have received their first book, encourage them to create more and send them into the setting to share with everyone.

What's in it for the parents?

This is an enjoyable activity for parents and will hopefully give them ideas for how to create many more books that they can share with their children.

Harry's summer holidays 2012

Sound of the week

What you need:

- A display table
- Laminated alphabet cards

What to do:

1. Choose a sound of the week and post it on the parents' noticeboard.

2. Ask parents to help their children find an object at home that begins with this sound.

3. Each day set aside some time to look at new objects with the group and add them to a display table.

Taking it forward

- Introduce a number and colour of the week and invite contributions toward similar displays.

What's in it for the parents?

Asking parents to contribute toward displays gives them direct involvement in daily activities creating a link between learning in the setting and at home.

Story time

What you need:

- Parents willing to read to your children

What to do:

1. Invite parents in to read to the children. Depending on how confident the parent is, they might like to sit in the book corner and share books with individuals and small groups. Or they may be happy to read to the whole group.

Taking it forward

- Ask parents what their favourite stories were as a child. Invite them to bring the stories in and read them to the children.

- Invite parents to help their children choose their favourite stories from home and send them in to be read at story time.

- For Reception age children, invite parents in to listen to individuals reading their reading books.

What's in it for the parents?

Sharing stories is an essential aspect of early learning and parents are an extremely valuable resource in this respect. Helping out will make them feel valued by practitioners and will be much appreciated by the children.

Special guests

What you need:

- Parents available to talk about their professional life

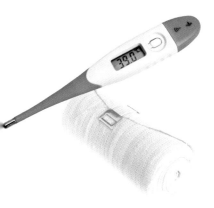

What to do:

1. Invite parents in to talk about their jobs and professions.

2. Provide them with guidance. Suggest, for instance, that they:

   - Think about how they can communicate their job in child-friendly terms.

   - Are accompanied by a special guest, for example a puppet or cuddly toy that can help explain the job.

   - Bring in interesting items they use at work.

   - Bring in photos of their work place.

3. Prepare the children for their visitor. Help them to research the profession and think of some questions to ask

Taking it forward

- Arrange with parents to visit some of their work places.

- Send a significant puppet or cuddly toy from the setting into a parent's work place along with a digital camera. Ask the parent to take photos of the puppet undertaking various aspects of their job, annotate the pictures and send them back in with the puppet to show the children.

- Create a display featuring parents' jobs and careers.

- Set up the role-play area to feature the various parents' work places the children learn about.

What's in it for the children?

Activities like this help everyone get to know each other, building a sense of community.

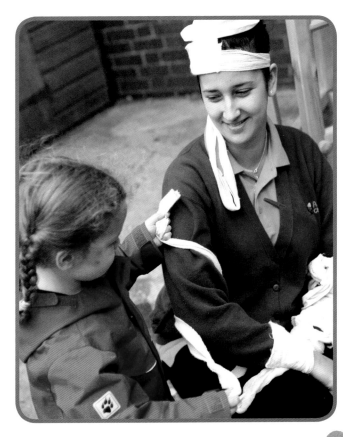

Family pets

What you need:

- Parents willing to bring in a family pet
- Book about pets

What to do:

1. Ask parents if they would be able to bring their family pet into the setting.

2. Prepare the children for the visit by researching the type of animal to find out, for example, where it lives, what it eats and how it might react to meeting a large group of noisy children.

3. Ask the child who owns the pet to tell everyone a bit about it, including how it likes to be handled.

4. Help the children prepare questions that they can ask the parent and child owners of the pet.

5. On the day of the visit bring the children together to meet the pet. Invite the parent to tell the children about the pet and answer any questions they might have.

✚ Health & Safety

- Find out if any children in the class have allergies and seek the advice of their parents before letting them have contact with animals.

- Meet the pet and assess how well it will cope with being among young children before you allow it to come into the setting.

- Ensure the children wash their hands after touching the pet.

Taking it forward

- Keep a pet in your setting and send it home at weekends to families on a rotational basis. Find comprehensive advice about keeping a pet in a setting at **http://www. nationalpetmonth.org.uk/ schools/** and **http://www.pdsa. org.uk/about-us/education/ pets-in-schools**.

- Make a diary for the pet for parents to fill in with their children.

What's in it for the parents?

This is another valuable learning experience that parents can make possible. Activities such as this affirm the parents' partnership role.

Helping out

What you need:

- Parent volunteers
- Written guidance on your policies
- A copy of your planning sheet

Taking it forward

- Organise a training workshop for new parent volunteers.

- Ask more established parents if they could work alongside new parents and help them settle in.

What's in it for the parents?

Giving parents such a valuable role puts them at the centre of the setting. Practitioners can learn from parental input and parents can learn about early education and child development.

Note

Parents should be made aware that they should not share their observations and opinions of children with other parents. It is a good idea to ask parent helpers to sign a confidentiality agreement.

What to do:

1. Invite parents into the setting to play and work with the children.

2. Before new parents begin, take time to talk about expectations. For example:
   - What they should do if a child needs help with toileting.
   - Who the various staff members are and what they are responsible for.
   - Why it is important to follow the daily routine.
   - What to do if they are experiencing difficulties relating to a child's behaviour.

3. Provide them with some written guidance explaining all of the above.

4. Show them a copy of the planning and explain how it works.

5. Give them copies of the setting's policies to read, including the child protection and health and safety policies.

6. Ask them what they feel most comfortable doing and if there is anything they would rather not do.

Odd jobs

What you need:

- Parent volunteers

What to do:

1. Post an advert on the parents' noticeboard asking for help with everyday jobs and administrative tasks including:

   - photocopying
   - laminating
   - cleaning equipment
   - repairing books
   - setting out resources
   - tidying out cupboards
   - replenishing art and craft resources
   - changing reading books
   - shopping for and preparing snack.

2. Be flexible with those parents who respond. Some may be able to come in at the same time every day or week. Others might be available at random times.

Taking it forward

- As parents grow in confidence and get to know the staff and children, invite them to take on tasks that involve working with individual children. Gradually build on this and encourage them to do more.

What's in it for the parents?

Not all parents have the confidence to play and work with children in the setting. Asking for their help with everyday jobs and administrative tasks is a good way of including them in other ways. This type of help is always very much appreciated by practitioners and so will give such parents a sense of value and purpose.

Sharing talents and expertise

What you need:

- Parents willing to share a skill

Taking it forward

- Think of activities that parents and children can work on together that would benefit the local community. For example, making kneelers for the local church, baking cakes for a charity bake sale, building bird boxes for a nature reserve or singing to the residents of a nursing home.

- Organise a talent show, where parents can show off interesting skills, such as singing, playing musical instruments, juggling or doing impressions. Encourage practitioners to join in too.

What's in it for the parents?

Giving parents this central role within the setting is a good way of broadening learning experiences for the children. Parents may be able to offer the children access to activities that practitioners might not otherwise have the knowledge, skills and confidence to deliver.

What to do:

1. Invite parents in to share their knowledge and skills with the children. Activities could include:

   - mural painting in the outdoor area
   - baking
   - cross stitch tapestry
   - woodwork
   - music
   - photography
   - sport.

2. Plan the activities with the parents beforehand. Think about the resources you will need, how many children can take part at a time and if the parents would benefit from the help of a support assistant.

Dad's and Mum's days

What you need:

- Time and staffing arrangements for a weekend activity
- Resources related to the particular activities planned
- Food and drinks

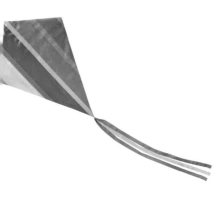

What to do:

1. Invite fathers in for a 'Dad's Day' and mothers in for a 'Mum's Day'. Organise these as separate events that are exclusive to fathers or mothers.

2. Plan the events for a Saturday or Sunday to give as many parents a chance to attend as possible.

3. Give each day a focus, taking into consideration the types of activities that will attract the different sexes. Some ideas include:
   - kite making
   - tree planting and gardening
   - bird box making
   - mural painting
   - large scale collaging
   - painting and decorating
   - baking
   - radio control car racing.

4. Cook lunch for everyone, have a BBQ or a picnic.

Taking it forward

- Try to organise a 'Dad's Day' and 'Mum's Day' at least once a term.
- Ask parents and children for activity ideas for future days.
- Set up a display showing photos from the days captioned with comments from the parents and children.

What's in it for the parents?

The purpose of arranging such days is to be as inclusive as possible by offering social events that will attract both fathers and mothers. Fathers are under-represented in the early years and making the effort to organise events that are planned specifically for them will help to make them feel more welcome.

A trip out

What to do:

1. Plan a trip to an outdoor location and invite parents to come along.

2. While on the trip, set a challenge that parents and children can work on together. Some examples are:

   - **woodland:** build a den for animals or people
   - **beach:** make a sandcastle or build a dam
   - **local park:** go on a scavenger hunt or run races
   - **stream/pond:** make a boat out of natural objects
   - **farm/zoo:** complete an animal quiz
   - **playground:** create a floor mural using natural objects.

3. Ask parents to bring along a picnic and sit down to eat together at lunchtime.

Taking it forward

- Ask parents to bring digital cameras on the trip. Set a homework task for them to use their photos to make a book about the visit.
- Create a display about the trip using photos contributed by the parents.

What's in it for the parents?

Setting a challenge when out on a day trip is a good way to move parents from a supervisory role to an interactive one. In addition, setting up group challenges helps them to forge relationships with other families.

Sports day

What you need:

- Sports equipment
- Trophies
- Rosettes

What to do:

1. Invite parents in for a sports day.

2. Ask parents for ideas for events. Involve them in planning the day and invite them in to help you set up.

Some suggestions for sports events are:

- obstacle race
- egg and spoon race
- throwing balls into buckets
- balancing beanbags on heads race
- Wellington boot throwing
- parent and child race
- jelly relay race
- dressing-up race.

3. On the day award trophies to the winners and rosettes to the runners-up.

Taking it forward

- Have a BBQ to round off the day.

- Plan some light-hearted 'parent only' events to bring parents together. For example, five-a-side football, tug-of-war, relay race, three-legged race and wheelbarrow race.

- Take photos of the event and create a display, or upload the pictures to the website for parents and children to view and share with their families.

What's in it for the parents?

This is a fun community-building event that parents can help to plan, organise and participate in.

Festival fun

What you need:

- Suitable items depending on the festival or special occasion you are celebrating

What to do:

1. Invite parents into the setting to celebrate festivals and special occasions. For example:

   - **Mother's/Father's Day:** make lunch.
   - **Easter:** set up an Easter egg hunt for younger siblings.
   - **Christmas:** organise a Christmas market.
   - **Chinese New Year:** perform a dragon dance.
   - **Jewish Passover festival:** act out the story of the Passover.
   - **Muslim festival of Eid ul-Fitr:** prepare a feast to celebrate the end of Ramadan.
   - **Hindu festival of Diwali:** decorate the setting with diva lamps and invite parents in to share sweets.

   For more ideas see *The Little Book of Special Days* (Featherstone).

2. Teach the children about the festival. Share stories and find out about traditions and rituals. Ask children to share their experiences of celebrating with their families at home.

3. Involve the children in planning and setting up the event. For example, help them to make Easter eggs, construct a large dragon, prepare food and make sweets. Help them to make invitations to send out.

4. Enjoy the celebrations.

Taking it forward

■ Ask the children and parents for suggestions about what kind of celebrations and events to plan.

■ Invite parents in to offer advice and help with the preparations.

■ Ask parents if they would be happy to come in and teach the children some traditional songs and rhymes linked to the festivals and celebrations.

What's in it for the parents?

This is another activity that helps to build a sense of community by inviting parents into the setting to socialise and celebrate together. Ensuring that you celebrate the festivals and special occasions that represent the various faiths and beliefs of all the children that attend your setting, helps to create cohesion.

Community garden

What you need:

- Outdoor space
- Plants and seeds
- Pots, planters and troughs
- Compost
- Gardening equipment for adults and children
- Parents interested in gardening or just willing to get involved

What to do:

1. Write to parents explaining that you plan to set up a community garden and invite them to an initial planning meeting.

2. Use the initial meeting to:
   - find out what the parents know and what skills they can offer
   - ask if any parents can donate equipment or plants
   - enquire if anyone has any contacts who might be able to help
   - look at the space you have and plan the layout of the garden
   - divide up tasks and allocate jobs
   - agree on a date for the first garden working party day.

3. On the first garden working party day bring practitioners, parents and children together to create and plant the garden.

4. Incorporate the tending of the garden into the setting's daily routine. Take working groups of children out each day to water the plants, weed the beds and keep everything tidy.

Taking it forward

- Invite the parents to come and tend the garden at any time.

- Hold regular working party days where everyone comes together to keep the garden going.

- Grow vegetables, use them to prepare a meal and invite the parents in to share it.

What's in it for the children?

Creating a community garden brings everyone together. Furthermore, for those parents who may not feel comfortable helping in the setting it offers an alternative way of getting involved.

Celebration assembly

What you need:

- Something that represents an achievement of each child in the setting, for example, an observation, photo or a piece of work
- Certificates

What to do:

1. Invite parents in to an assembly to celebrate their children's achievements.

2. Before the assembly, teach the children some songs linked to the current theme or time of year, that they can perform for parents.

3. Create a display of observations, photos and pieces of work for parents to look at on their way in and out.

4. During the assembly bring children out to the front to receive certificates in celebration of what they have done.

Taking it forward

- After the assembly, serve hot drinks, cakes and biscuits (which can be prepared by the children) and take time to chat with parents.

- Hold regular celebration assemblies once or twice a term.

- Each week nominate a child who has achieved something special to be 'star of the week'. To mark the occasion, give the child a little bear to take home. Give the bear a little rucksack and inside put a treat and a miniature certificate to explain to parents why their child is star of the week.

What's in it for the children?

Celebration assemblies are social occasions that bring practitioners and parents together to praise the children's achievements.

Parent-setting association

What you need:

- Time to hold regular meetings
- Volunteer parents

What to do:

1. Set up a parent-setting association where volunteer parent members can take an active role in the management of the setting.

2. Elect a parent governor.

3. Hold regular meetings and involve the parents in:
   - planning and organising fundraising events
   - planning and organising social events
   - writing and reviewing policies
   - planning outings and visits
   - planning and reviewing themes, topics and projects.

We went to Lyme Park and I dug in the sand with the big digger.

Taking it forward

- Involve parents in producing information leaflets or planning and organising information evenings to show what the association does with the aim of enthusing other parents.

What's in it for the parents?

A parent-setting association puts parents at the heart of the organisation and management of the setting. It is a way that practitioners can demonstrate that they recognise and value the role that parents play in their children's learning and development.

Extra-curricular classes

What you need:

- Contacts who are able to run extra-curricular classes
- Space to hold the classes

What to do:

1. Organise extra-curricular classes for parents. Some ideas include:
   - jewellery making
   - aerobics
   - cookery
   - first aid
   - adult literacy and numeracy
   - computer skills
   - furniture restoration
   - photography.

2. Ask parents when they are most likely to attend such classes, if they have any suggestions for types of class and how much they would be prepared to pay.

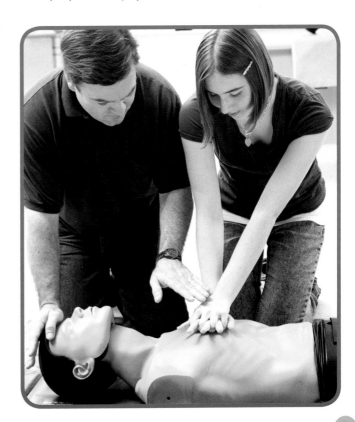

Taking it forward

- Find out if there are any parents who have particular skills and feel they would be able to take on running a class.

What's in it for the parents?

Organising extra-curricular classes not only provides the opportunity to learn new skills, it brings parents together, helping them to forge friendships. What's more, practical classes are great for parents who speak English as an additional language.

Note

Consider the costs involved in arranging extra-curricular activities. If the class is too expensive it may automatically exclude a large number of parents.

Observations at home

What you need:

- Digital cameras and video cameras
- Parents' email addresses
- Example photo observations

What to do:

1. Provide parents with digital cameras and video cameras. A useful durable resource is the Digital Blue camera: **www.digitalblue.org.uk**.

2. Provide them with examples of photo observations of their child taken in the setting.

3. Send an accompanying letter explaining that you would like them to use the cameras to take some photos or film of their children playing at home. Ask them to email the photos to you. Invite them to provide supporting notes explaining what the activity is and any thoughts or comments they might have about what their child is doing and learning. Invite them to include any questions they might have and ask them if there are any areas where they feel their child needs development.

4. Reply to the email with your own comments about the observation and offer suggestions and responses to questions.

Top tip

Check if parents have their own cameras they can use. Otherwise disposable cameras are just as effective if you are concerned about sending expensive equipment home.

Taking it forward

- Email observations taken in the setting to parents and ask for their comments and feedback.

- Provide paper templates for parents to record handwritten observations if they are uncomfortable using a digital camera or computer.

- Encourage verbal feedback from parents who are unable to write or use a computer.

- Set up meetings with parents to go through and discuss the observations together.

What's in it for the parents?

Involving parents in observation educates them about assessment procedures in the EYFS and helps them to learn more about their children and the value of play. What's more, email is quick, convenient and free, offering practitioners the opportunity to keep parents regularly updated about their children's progress.

Note

Ensure parents are aware that they should only be taking photos and film of their own children. They should not email pictures or footage of other children who happen to be around at the time.

Curriculum workshops

What you need:

- Initial planning ideas for a topic or project
- Ideas and suggestions from the children

Taking it forward

- Reach out to parents who are unable to attend a workshop by sending out letters, with a reply slip, asking for any ideas they might have or help they may be able to offer.

- Find out from parents if they know anyone in the local community who might be able to come in and offer any skills or knowledge.

- Keep parents informed. As the topic or project progresses send home regular updates about what is happening.

What's in it for the parents?

Inviting parents to curriculum workshops builds a sense of partnership. It sends the message that parents' ideas are welcome and their knowledge and skills are valued. It also affirms their position as their children's first and foremost educators.

Top tip ★

Try to hold the workshop well in advance of the start of the topic or project. This will enable parents to plan ahead and make themselves available to help.

What to do:

1. Invite parents to come into the setting for a planning workshop.

2. Share the initial planning ideas and ask the parents if they have any ideas to add.

3. Find out if any of the parents have any particular skills or knowledge that they can offer. Do they have any ideas for activities they might be able to help with or resources they can get hold of through their work or people they know?